The
Twelve Days
of
Christmas

igloobooks

How Many?

In the Christmas song, how many of each thing is mentioned?
Fill in the missing numbers and find the missing stickers.

1 partridge in a pear tree

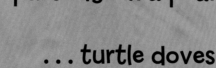

. . . turtle doves

3 french hens

4 calling birds

. . . gold rings

6 geese-a-laying

7 swans-a-swimming

. . . maids-a-milking

9 ladies dancing

. . . lords-a-leaping

11 pipers piping

12 drummers drumming

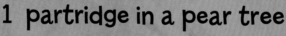

Moving Pictures

You will need:
A small circle of card
2 short pieces of string
A hole punch

step 5

Instructions:

step 1. Stick a sticker of a partridge onto one side of your card.

step 2. Turn over the card and stick a pear tree onto the other side, making sure the stickers are opposite ways up and in the centre.

step 3. Punch a hole in each side of the circle, as shown in the picture.

step 4. Now tie a small piece of string through each of the holes and tie a knot in the end.

step 5. Grab the ends of the string and twirl.

Now here's the magic part, it looks like the partridge is in the pear tree!

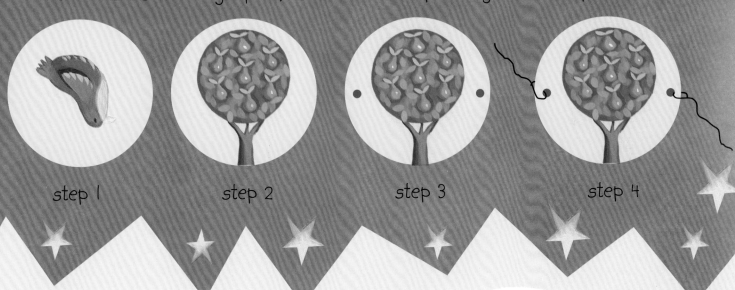

step 1   step 2   step 3   step 4

Drawing Fun

Draw a partridge in a pear tree by following the lines.

How many pears can you count in the tree?

Dove Decorations

Make some turtle dove decorations to hang on your Christmas tree.

You will need:
White card
Thin ribbon, or cotton
Scissors
Felt-tip pens

Instructions:

1. Trace the turtle dove and its wings, as shown, onto your white card.

2. With the help of an adult, cut out your turtle dove and wing shape. Make the hole and a thin slit where shown.

3. Draw eyes on either side of the head with the felt-tip pen.

4. Fold the wings along the dotted lines and push through the slot in the body (**fig a**), then fold the wings back down again to lock the wings into place (**fig b**).

5. Slot some thin ribbon, or cotton through the hole. Tie it in a knot, or bow.

6. Decorate your turtle dove in any way you wish and hang on your tree.

fig a

fig b

What's Missing?

Can you spot what each hen is missing?

a.

b.

c.

Which Way Home?

The calling birds are singing to help their friend get back to the nest. Which route leads him there?

a.

b.

c.

Gold Rings

Each of these rings belongs to a matching pair.
Can you find the ring that doesn't match any of the others?
Match each ring to it's pair and there will be only one left.

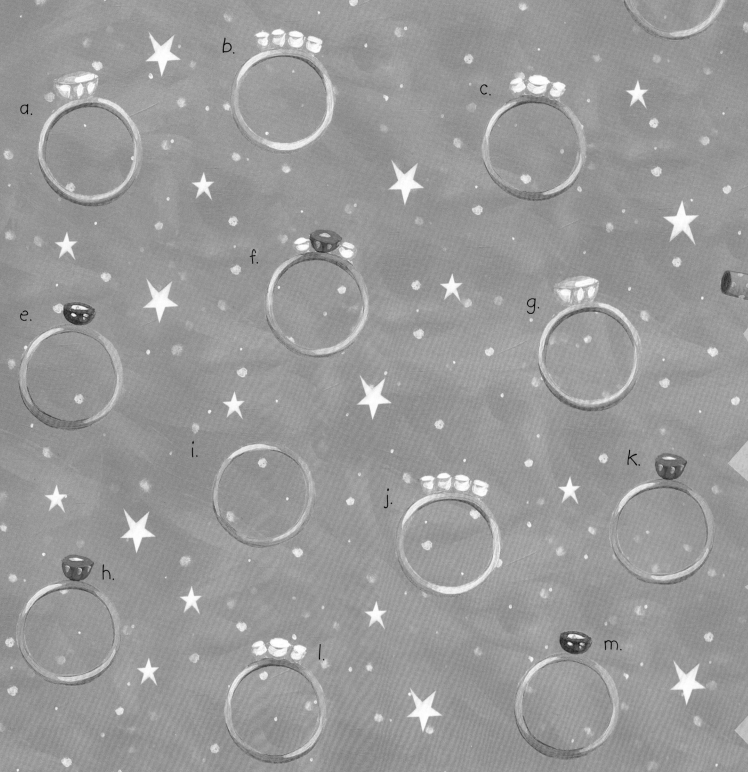

a.

b.

c.

d.

e.

f.

g.

h.

i.

j.

k.

l.

m.

Hidden Rings

There are 5 gold rings hidden on the tree in this picture. Can you spot them all?

Goosey, Goosey

Find the correct sticker to match the number of eggs each goose has laid.
Then count the eggs and see which goose has laid the most.

a.

b.

c.

d.

e.

f.

Christmas Chase

Play this game with your friends.
Each player chooses a different sticker, from
the book and sticks it onto a coin. These will be
your counters and should be placed on the 'START'
star. Then take it in turns to roll the dice and
move round the board. The first to the parcel wins.

4 Stop to feed the calling birds. Go back 1 space.

5

3

START

2

1

22 Help the maids milk the cows. Go back 1 space.

21

23

24

25

26

27

28

29 Stop to collect the eggs. Miss a go.

30

31

32

33

Christmas Decorations

Tie a piece of thin string through
the hole at the top of each
decoration, as shown.
Then hang them on your tree.
See if you and your friends can
find all twelve of them.

How Many?

Goosey, Goosey

What's Missing?

Swimming Swans

The seven swans are swimming through the reeds. Trace the path with your finger. Then draw along the dotted line with a pen or a pencil.

Odd Ones Out

Not all of the birds shown here are in the twelve days of Christmas song.
Can you spot the odd ones out?

d.

e.

h.

j.

k.

b.

i.

f.

a.

c.

g.

l.

Answers: Odd Ones Out: c, e, g, j, k, l

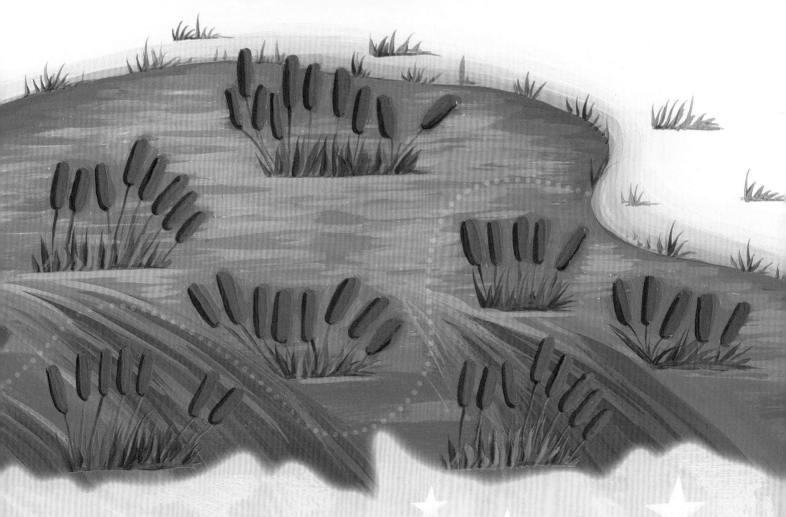

Down in the Dairy

The maids are about to start milking the cows.
Circle the things they will need.

a.

b.

c.

d.

e.

f.

g.

Dancing Ladies

Make some beautfiul dancing ladies to hang up in your house at Christmas time.

You will need:

White card
Cotton thread
Scissors
A pencil

Instructions:

1. Trace the dancer onto card 9 times.
2. With the help of an adult, cut out your dancer shapes and make the holes where shown.
3. Thread the cotton through the holes on each dancer and line them up with their hands touching. Allow enough cotton at each end so you can hold it.
4. Decorate the 9 dancers in any way you wish.
5. You can now make all the dancers dance by gently pulling the cotton tight and waving the cotton. Or you can hang them up.

Find a Pair of Pipers

Which two pipers are exactly the same?

a.　　b.　　c.　　d.　　e.　　f.

Leaping Lords

Join the dots to complete the picture.
Now count how many leaping lords there are.

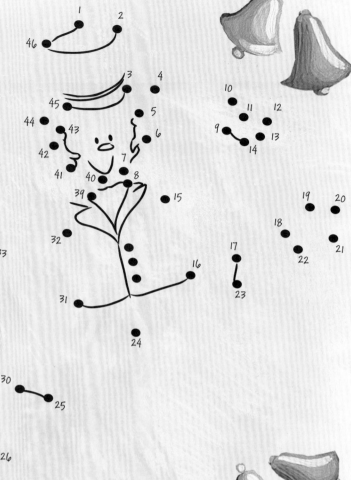

1
2
46
3
4
45
44
43
5
42
6
41
40
7
39
8
32
15
31
24
38
36
33
37 35 34
30
25
29
26
28
27
10
11 12
9
13
14
19 20
18
21
22
17
16
23

g.
h.
i.
j.
k.

Double Drummers

Can you shade the drummer to make him exactly the same as the other eleven?

Shake, Rattle and Roll

Can you say the names of the instruments below?
Have some fun trying to make the sound of each one.

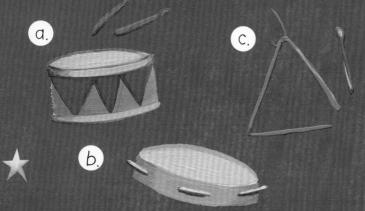

a.

b.

c.

d.

e.

What's Missing?

Each of these pictures is missing something.
Find a sticker to complete each one.

Memory Test

Look at the picture below for a few minutes.
Then close the book and try to remember what was on the page.